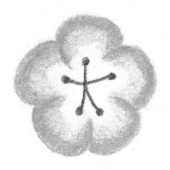

GETTING READY

Your Journal to Help You
Deal with and Heal from Sexual Harassment

Sara Jones

Plum Blossom Creations, LLC
San Diego, CA
www.plumblossomcreations.com

Copyright © 2018 by Sara Jones

Published by Plum Blossom Creations, LLC
P.O. Box 235146
Encinitas, CA 92024

Cover Illustration: Sara Jones
Cover Design: Sara Jones
Typography: Sara Jones
Back Cover Photo: Kimberly Tilton

Library of Congress Cataloguing-in-Publication Data

Sara Jones, 2018 - Getting Ready: Your Journal to Help You Deal with and Heal from Sexual Harassment

ISBN-13: 978-0-692-09914-8

Printed in the United States
Distributed by Plum Blossom Creations, LLC

Always, in all ways, invest in Bloom.

♡ Sara

Table of Contents

Introduction

Summing Up

"Que sera, sera."
Doris Day

The Doability Doctrine
"Where our interests are clear, our values are at stake
and we can make a difference, we must act, and we must lead."
Madeleine Albright

" —the readiness is all."
William Shakespeare, *Hamlet*, Act 5, Scene 2

~

Life happens. Though we hope it goes well, sometimes it doesn't.

Sometimes, the person sexually harassing you is unaware that his or her actions are offensive, perhaps even illegal. With these people, we have the opportunity to lead. We have the opportunity to actively maintain our values. We also have the opportunity to help these people become aware of their offenses and to offer them the opportunity to choose to learn a new way of behaving.

Sometimes, the person harassing you is fully aware that his or her actions are offensive, perhaps even illegal. With these people, we have the same opportunity to lead.

In either case, we have a choice. We can choose to act out of ignorance or maliciousness, as they have done. Or we can choose to act gracefully and humanely. The former draws us away from our true selves and the latter helps us to live into our true selves.

To lead ourselves and others well, we must be in full bloom. We must be ready in all five petals of our being – physical, emotional, social, intellectual, and spiritual.

To be ready to lead, we must anticipate some of life's more challenging moments, explore the spectrum of possible reactions to them and then reflect on how those actions positively and negatively impact ourselves and others.

This Journal offers you 52 scenarios related to sexual harassment in the workplace, one for every week. With each scenario, you will be prompted to explore the thoughts, words and actions that you could take that would pull you away from your most beautiful self and which thoughts, words and actions keep you in full bloom.

Your answers will help you learn more about yourself. They will help you know how ready you are to deal with each scenario and in which of the five petals you still need to grow.

Find 2 or 3 friends to go on this journal journey with you. Once a quarter, or after every 12 weeks, you are invited to pause your introspection and reconnect with those in your trusted circle. Plan a meal together, host a Gathering and open up about your "Getting Ready" experience. How are you all doing with your journaling? Where are you finding yourselves being ready? Where are you needing some growth? Do you have some growth areas in common? Can someone's strengths help someone else grow?

Take this slow. Go at a comfortable pace. Be gentle with yourself and with each other.

Staying true to your values and your integrity, when those around you want you to compromise them, can bring conflict. But, by anticipating how to react to any one scenario before it occurs, you can stay in full bloom while helping yourself and others grow. Then maybe one day, perhaps you can anticipate how to avoid the scenario altogether.

This work is not easy. You will find you have some strengths already. You might also find that you are weak in some areas and that can be difficult to handle. You might make a mistake or two but invest in the process of getting ready. Trust that over time, and with practice, as these decision points rise up to meet you, there will come a day when you will already know what to do. And that is success.

So, choose a day once a week (I choose Sundays) to find a quiet hour to sit in your favorite mediation spot. Have a glass of water (or wine!) at your elbow and focus on you and your five petals.

Always, in always, invest in Bloom.
Sara Jones
San Diego, CA, 2018

"So, learn from this, better yourself
and you will be better for next time."

Meredith Grey
"How to Save a Life", *Grey's Anatomy*
Season 11 Episode 21

Week 1

Scenario #1: You are in a meeting with 7 other people of mixed genders. The male leader at the table says, "Let's lift the skirt on this project proposal and see if it has legs."

What could you think, say or do in this situation, to all those involved, that would pull you away from being your very best self?

The Victim	
Witnesses	
The Harasser	
HR/Supervisor	

What could you think, say or do in this situation, to all those involved, that would enable you to fully bloom?

 The Victim	
 Witnesses	
 The Harasser	
HR/Supervisor	

What knowledge, skills and abilities (K.S.A.s) do you have already, and which do you need to learn, acquire and grow to be your best self in this scenario?

"Stand by while atrocities are taking place
and you're an accomplice."

C.J. Cregg
"Inauguration: Over There", *The West Wing*
Season 4, Episode 15

Week 2

Scenario #2: You are out playing paintball in a team-building exercise. Three of the men gang up on you and use your buttocks as a bulls-eye. They pelt you over and over again, laughing heartily.

What could you think, say or do in this situation, to all those involved, that would pull you away from being your very best self?

The Victim	
Witnesses	
The Harasser	
HR/Supervisor	

What could you think, say or do in this situation, to all those involved, that would enable you to fully bloom?

The Victim	
Witnesses	
The Harasser	
HR/Supervisor	

What knowledge, skills and abilities (K.S.A.s) do you have already, and which do you need to learn, acquire and grow to be your best self in this scenario?

"Strong is Vader. Mind what you have learned. Save it you can."

Yoda
Star Wars: Episode V – The Empire Strikes Back

Week 3

Scenario #3: A male colleague and you are vying for the same promotion. Your colleague butters up with the supervisor by going to happy hours, lunches and cracking jokes with him. You're not included.

What could you think, say or do in this situation, to all those involved, that would pull you away from being your very best self?

The Victim	
Witnesses	
The Harasser	
HR/Supervisor	

What could you think, say or do in this situation, to all those involved, that would enable you to fully bloom?

The Victim	
Witnesses	
The Harasser	
HR/Supervisor	

What knowledge, skills and abilities (K.S.A.s) do you have already, and which do you need to learn, acquire and grow to be your best self in this scenario?

"If you don't know where you're going,
you will probably end up somewhere else."

Laurence J. Peter
Peter's Quotations: Ideas for Our Time

Week 4

Scenario #4: You and a male colleague both have the potential for moving up in the company. One of you may become the other person's supervisor one day. He asks you out on a date.

What could you think, say or do in this situation, to all those involved, that would pull you away from being your very best self?

The Victim	
Witnesses	
The Harasser	
HR/Supervisor	

What could you think, say or do in this situation, to all those involved, that would enable you to fully bloom?

The Victim	
Witnesses	
The Harasser	
HR/Supervisor	

What knowledge, skills and abilities (K.S.A.s) do you have already, and which do you need to learn, acquire and grow to be your best self in this scenario?

"It takes courage to grow up and become who you really are."

e. e. cummings
Poet

Week 5

Scenario #5: A female colleague sits a little too close to you in meetings and laughs just a little too heartily at your jokes.

What could you think, say or do in this situation, to all those involved, that would pull you away from being your very best self?

The Victim	
Witnesses	
The Harasser	
HR/Supervisor	

What could you think, say or do in this situation, to all those involved, that would enable you to fully bloom?

The Victim	
Witnesses	
The Harasser	
HR/Supervisor	

What knowledge, skills and abilities (K.S.A.s) do you have already, and which do you need to learn, acquire and grow to be your best self in this scenario?

"Do not follow where the path may lead.
Go, instead, where there is no path and leave a trail."

Ralph Waldo Emerson
Essayist, Lecturer, Philosopher and Poet

Week 6

Scenario #6: You're in a new town. You just relocated for this new job. The other women in the office take you out to lunch and warn you about the wandering hands of your boss. The next day you understand why, first hand.

What could you think, say or do in this situation, to all those involved, that would pull you away from being your very best self?

The Victim	
Witnesses	
The Harasser	
HR/Supervisor	

What could you think, say or do in this situation, to all those involved, that would enable you to fully bloom?

The Victim	
Witnesses	
The Harasser	
HR/Supervisor	

What knowledge, skills and abilities (K.S.A.s) do you have already, and which do you need to learn, acquire and grow to be your best self in this scenario?

"There are no shortcuts to any place worth going."

Beverly Sills
Singer, Opera Star

Week 7

Scenario #7: One of your male colleagues who you think has a crush on you, puts a big smile on his face and offers to put your name in the hat for the next project lead if you help him work the numbers on this current project for the budget office.

What could you think, say or do in this situation, to all those involved, that would pull you away from being your very best self?

The Victim	
Witnesses	
The Harasser	
HR/Supervisor	

What could you think, say or do in this situation, to all those involved, that would enable you to fully bloom?

 The Victim	
Witnesses	
The Harasser	
HR/Supervisor	

What knowledge, skills and abilities (K.S.A.s) do you have already, and which do you need to learn, acquire and grow to be your best self in this scenario?

"What you leave behind is not what is engraved in stone monuments, but what is woven into the lives of others."

Pericles
Greek Statement, Orator and General

Week 8

Scenario #8: The team decides to get together for a meal at one of your homes. You decide as a group that you want lasagna. They all look at you when the question comes up, "Who's gonna bake it?"

What could you think, say or do in this situation, to all those involved, that would pull you away from being your very best self?

The Victim	
Witnesses	
The Harasser	
HR/Supervisor	

What could you think, say or do in this situation, to all those involved, that would enable you to fully bloom?

The Victim	
Witnesses	
The Harasser	
HR/Supervisor	

What knowledge, skills and abilities (K.S.A.s) do you have already, and which do you need to learn, acquire and grow to be your best self in this scenario?

"I can't change the direction of the wind,
but I can adjust my sails to always reach my destination."

Jimmy Dean
Country Music Artist, TV Host, Businessman

Week 9

Scenario #9: You and a male colleague get along very well socially as well as professionally. A jealous male colleague accuses you in the breakroom of having an affair.

What could you think, say or do in this situation, to all those involved, that would pull you away from being your very best self?

The Victim	
Witnesses	
The Harasser	
HR/Supervisor	

What could you think, say or do in this situation, to all those involved, that would enable you to fully bloom?

The Victim	
Witnesses	
The Harasser	
HR/Supervisor	

What knowledge, skills and abilities (K.S.A.s) do you have already, and which do you need to learn, acquire and grow to be your best self in this scenario?

"Start by doing what's necessary; then do what's possible; and suddenly you are doing the impossible."

Saint Francis of Assisi
Catholic Friar, Deacon, and Preacher

Week 10

Scenario #10: You're the only woman on a 10-person team. The others tease you daily about this 1:9 ratio. "Do you ever get lonely?" "Which one of us do you like the best?"

What could you think, say or do in this situation, to all those involved, that would pull you away from being your very best self?

The Victim	
Witnesses	
The Harasser	
HR/Supervisor	

What could you think, say or do in this situation, to all those involved, that would enable you to fully bloom?

The Victim	
Witnesses	
The Harasser	
HR/Supervisor	

What knowledge, skills and abilities (K.S.A.s) do you have already, and which do you need to learn, acquire and grow to be your best self in this scenario?

"Change your thoughts and you change the world."

Norman Vincente Peale
Minister, Author

Week 11

Scenario #11: You're one of a handful of women in a military unit. One of the men in your unit teases you, "Are you women on the same menstrual cycle yet?"

What could you think, say or do in this situation, to all those involved, that would pull you away from being your very best self?

The Victim	
Witnesses	
The Harasser	
HR/Supervisor	

What could you think, say or do in this situation, to all those involved, that would enable you to fully bloom?

The Victim	
Witnesses	
The Harasser	
HR/Supervisor	

What knowledge, skills and abilities (K.S.A.s) do you have already, and which do you need to learn, acquire and grow to be your best self in this scenario?

"No act of kindness, no matter how small, is ever wasted."

Aesop
Greek Fabulist, Storyteller

Week 12

Scenario #12: At each other's desks, in the hallways chatting, everywhere but in meetings with others, one of your colleagues repeatedly reaches out to touch you and lingers just a little too long for your comfort, every time.

What could you think, say or do in this situation, to all those involved, that would pull you away from being your very best self?

The Victim	
Witnesses	
The Harasser	
HR/Supervisor	

What could you think, say or do in this situation, to all those involved, that would enable you to fully bloom?

The Victim	
Witnesses	
The Harasser	
HR/Supervisor	

What knowledge, skills and abilities (K.S.A.s) do you have already, and which do you need to learn, acquire and grow to be your best self in this scenario?

"Never doubt that a small group of thoughtful, committed citizens can change the world; indeed, it's the only thing that ever has."

Margaret Mead
Cultural Anthropologist, Author, Speaker

Gathering

Find 2 or 3 friends to go on this journal journey with you.
Once a quarter, or after every 12 weeks, I invite you to pause your
introspection and reconnect with those in your trusted circle.
Plan a meal together, host a Gathering and
open up about your "Getting Ready" experience so far.

Scenario #13a: How are you "ready" to deal with and heal from these scenarios – physically, emotionally, socially, intellectually, and spiritually? What KSAs have you mastered already?

Physical

Emotional

Social

Intellectual

Spiritual

Scenario #13b: In which petals do you still have some "getting ready" work to do? What are the common growth areas? Can someone's strengths help someone else grow? What is your plan for growth?

Physical

Emotional

Social

Intellectual

Spiritual

"The trick is, whether you win or lose, not to fail."

Meredith Grey
"The Distance", *Grey's Anatomy*
Season 11 Episode 14

Week 14

Scenario #14: You're a consultant in a critical meeting with a client. You cannot lose your cool. Both a colleague and your client, buddies, interrupt your presentation and mansplain a trivial point, distracting the focus away from your critical point in the presentation.

What could you think, say or do in this situation, to all those involved, that would pull you away from being your very best self?

The Victim	
Witnesses	
The Harasser	
HR/Supervisor	

What could you think, say or do in this situation, to all those involved, that would enable you to fully bloom?

The Victim	
Witnesses	
The Harasser	
HR/Supervisor	

What knowledge, skills and abilities (K.S.A.s) do you have already, and which do you need to learn, acquire and grow to be your best self in this scenario?

"There is a growing strength in women
but it's in the forehead, not the forearm."

Beverly Sills
Singer, Opera Star

Week 15

Scenario #15: You're a pilot. It's you and your co-pilot locked in the cockpit for a 6-hour flight. Your co-pilot, the captain, has been entertaining you with sexual jokes and a "who can come up with the worst pick-up line" contest.

What could you think, say or do in this situation, to all those involved, that would pull you away from being your very best self?

The Victim	
Witnesses	
The Harasser	
HR/Supervisor	

What could you think, say or do in this situation, to all those involved, that would enable you to fully bloom?

The Victim	

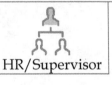 Witnesses	

The Harasser	

HR/Supervisor	

What knowledge, skills and abilities (K.S.A.s) do you have already, and which do you need to learn, acquire and grow to be your best self in this scenario?

"Every time we turn our heads the other way
when we see the law flouted,
when we tolerate what we know to be wrong,
when we close our eyes and ears to the corrupt
because we are too busy or too frightened,
when we fail to speak up and speak out,
we strike a blow against freedom and decency and justice."

Robert Kennedy
United States Senator and Lawyer

Week 16

Scenario #16: You are a new journalist assigned to the minor league baseball games. You enter the locker room for your first post-game interviews with the team.

What could you think, say or do in this situation, to all those involved, that would pull you away from being your very best self?

The Victim	
Witnesses	
The Harasser	
HR/Supervisor	

What could you think, say or do in this situation, to all those involved, that would enable you to fully bloom?

The Victim	
Witnesses	
The Harasser	
HR/Supervisor	

What knowledge, skills and abilities (K.S.A.s) do you have already, and which do you need to learn, acquire and grow to be your best self in this scenario?

"When you assume negative intent, you're angry.
If you take away that anger and assume positive intent,
you will be amazed. Your emotional quotient goes up because
you are no longer almost random in your response."

Indra Nooyi
Indian American Business Executive

Week 17

Scenario #17: You're a waitress at an all-night diner. The truckers and other motorists that stop have that lonely look about them.

What could you think, say or do in this situation, to all those involved, that would pull you away from being your very best self?

The Victim	
Witnesses	
The Harasser	
HR/Supervisor	

What could you think, say or do in this situation, to all those involved, that would enable you to fully bloom?

The Victim	
Witnesses	
The Harasser	
HR/Supervisor	

What knowledge, skills and abilities (K.S.A.s) do you have already, and which do you need to learn, acquire and grow to be your best self in this scenario?

"Life is 10% what happens to you and 90% how you react to it."

Charles R. Swindoll
Evangelical Christian Pastor, Author, Educator, and Radio Preacher

Week 18

Scenario #18: You are one of a handful of female cops in a 100-person precinct. On your first day, you find the women's locker room plastered with centerfolds.

What could you think, say or do in this situation, to all those involved, that would pull you away from being your very best self?

The Victim	
Witnesses	
The Harasser	
HR/Supervisor	

What could you think, say or do in this situation, to all those involved, that would enable you to fully bloom?

The Victim	
Witnesses	
The Harasser	
HR/Supervisor	

What knowledge, skills and abilities (K.S.A.s) do you have already, and which do you need to learn, acquire and grow to be your best self in this scenario?

"A leader is best when people barely know he exists,
when his work is done, his aim fulfilled, they will say:
we did it ourselves."

Lao Tzu
Ancient Chinese philosopher and writer,
reputed author of the *Tao Te Ching*

Week 19

Scenario #19: You're an MBA student at a job fair and the recruiter says he likes your resume and might have a job offer for you. He asks you to meet him at his hotel to talk about it over drinks and appetizers. His treat! He has an expense account.

What could you think, say or do in this situation, to all those involved, that would pull you away from being your very best self?

The Victim	
Witnesses	
The Harasser	
HR/Supervisor	

What could you think, say or do in this situation, to all those involved, that would enable you to fully bloom?

The Victim	
Witnesses	
The Harasser	
HR/Supervisor	

What knowledge, skills and abilities (K.S.A.s) do you have already, and which do you need to learn, acquire and grow to be your best self in this scenario?

"Be sure you put your feet in the right place, then stand firm."

Abraham Lincoln
American statesman and lawyer,
16th President of the United States (March, 1861- April, 1865)

Week 20

Scenario #20: You are a programmer at a new job and need to make a good impression. The other programmers are guys and they are shutting you out of the casual banter about new code tricks.

What could you think, say or do in this situation, to all those involved, that would pull you away from being your very best self?

The Victim	
Witnesses	
The Harasser	
HR/Supervisor	

What could you think, say or do in this situation, to all those involved, that would enable you to fully bloom?

The Victim	
Witnesses	
The Harasser	
HR/Supervisor	

What knowledge, skills and abilities (K.S.A.s) do you have already, and which do you need to learn, acquire and grow to be your best self in this scenario?

"It is the nature of mistakes that one causes another."

Erasmus of Rotterdam
Dutch Renaissance Humanist, Catholic Priest,
Social Critic, Teacher, and Theologian

Week 21

Scenario #21: You're a member of the women's basketball team at college. You're eating late in the cafeteria with the other sports teams. Three male athletes approach you and want to know what it's like being a butch.

What could you think, say or do in this situation, to all those involved, that would pull you away from being your very best self?

The Victim	
Witnesses	
The Harasser	
HR/Supervisor	

What could you think, say or do in this situation, to all those involved, that would enable you to fully bloom?

The Victim	
Witnesses	
The Harasser	
HR/Supervisor	

What knowledge, skills and abilities (K.S.A.s) do you have already, and which do you need to learn, acquire and grow to be your best self in this scenario?

"Be kind whenever possible. It is always possible."

Dalai Lama
Tibetan Buddhism Monk

Week 22

Scenario #22: You're a CEO at a retreat for professional CEOs. After dinner, you are all invited to the library for cigars and cognac. One member even breaks out his pipe.

What could you think, say or do in this situation, to all those involved, that would pull you away from being your very best self?

The Victim	
Witnesses	
The Harasser	
HR/Supervisor	

What could you think, say or do in this situation, to all those involved, that would enable you to fully bloom?

The Victim	
Witnesses	
The Harasser	
HR/Supervisor	

What knowledge, skills and abilities (K.S.A.s) do you have already, and which do you need to learn, acquire and grow to be your best self in this scenario?

"Though the sex to which I belong is considered weak
you will nevertheless find me a rock that bends to no wind."

Queen Elizabeth I
Queen of England and Ireland (November, 1558 – March, 1603)

Week 23

Scenario #23: You are the Queen of England and single. You are being courted for marriage by the leaders of two other foreign nations.

What could you think, say or do in this situation, to all those involved, that would pull you away from being your very best self?

The Victim	
Witnesses	
The Harasser	
HR/Supervisor	

What could you think, say or do in this situation, to all those involved, that would enable you to fully bloom?

The Victim	
Witnesses	
The Harasser	
HR/Supervisor	

What knowledge, skills and abilities (K.S.A.s) do you have already, and which do you need to learn, acquire and grow to be your best self in this scenario?

"I guess I've played a lot of victims,
but that's what a lot of the history of women is about."

Jodie Foster
American Actress, Director, and Producer

Week 24

Scenario #24: You are a struggling actress and have given yourself the ultimatum of getting the next gig or leaving the business. A director approaches you and offers you a role in his next film. You say yes and then he asks you to dinner at his place to celebrate.

What could you think, say or do in this situation, to all those involved, that would pull you away from being your very best self?

The Victim	
Witnesses	
The Harasser	
HR/Supervisor	

What could you think, say or do in this situation, to all those involved, that would enable you to fully bloom?

The Victim	
Witnesses	
The Harasser	
HR/Supervisor	

What knowledge, skills and abilities (K.S.A.s) do you have already, and which do you need to learn, acquire and grow to be your best self in this scenario?

"Sense the blessings of the earth
in the perfect arc of a ripe tangerine, the taste of warm, fresh bread, the
circling flight of birds, the lavender color of the sky shining in a late
afternoon rain puddle, the million times we pass other beings in our
cars and shops and out among the trees
without crashing, conflict, or harm."

Jack Kornfield
Bestselling Author and Teacher

Week 25

Scenario #25: You are a student of Massage Therapy. In one of your class sessions, your massage partner and classmate lightly brushes your breast while practicing his back massage techniques. You sense that he crossed the lines of intimacy far too easily, perhaps intentionally. But you are not sure.

What could you think, say or do in this situation, to all those involved, that would pull you away from being your very best self?

The Victim	
Witnesses	
The Harasser	
HR/Supervisor	

What could you think, say or do in this situation, to all those involved, that would enable you to fully bloom?

The Victim	
Witnesses	
The Harasser	
HR/Supervisor	

What knowledge, skills and abilities (K.S.A.s) do you have already, and which do you need to learn, acquire and grow to be your best self in this scenario?

"The mark of your ignorance is
the depth of your belief in injustice and tragedy.
What the caterpillar calls the end of the world,
the Master calls the butterfly."

Richard Bach
Author
Jonathan Livingston Seagull

Week 26

Scenario #26: You are a single mom with two school-age kids. You are an administrative assistant to the company executive. He stays late. You stay late. One night, after a particularly difficult day for him, he asks you into his office and kisses you. You resist. He forces it.

What could you think, say or do in this situation, to all those involved, that would pull you away from being your very best self?

The Victim	
Witnesses	
The Harasser	
HR/Supervisor	

What could you think, say or do in this situation, to all those involved, that would enable you to fully bloom?

The Victim	
Witnesses	
The Harasser	
HR/Supervisor	

What knowledge, skills and abilities (K.S.A.s) do you have already, and which do you need to learn, acquire and grow to be your best self in this scenario?

"I think there are things that we can all do to build resilience in ourselves, but also to build resilience in each other."

Sheryl Sandberg
Technology Executive, Activist, and Author

Gathering

Find 2 or 3 friends to go on this journal journey with you.
Once a quarter, or after every 12 weeks, I invite you to pause your
introspection and reconnect with those in your trusted circle.
Plan a meal together, host a Gathering and
open up about your "Getting Ready" experience so far.

Scenario #27a: How are you "ready" to deal with and heal from these scenarios – physically, emotionally, socially, intellectually, and spiritually? What KSAs have you mastered already?

Physical

Emotional

Social

Intellectual

Spiritual

Scenario #27b: In which petals do you still have some "getting ready" work to do? What are the common growth areas? Can someone's strengths help someone else grow? What is your plan for growth?

Physical

Emotional

Social

Intellectual

Spiritual

"If you want to nudge people into socially desirable behavior,
do not, by any means, let them know
that their current actions are better than the social norm."

Richard H. Thaler
Author
Nudge: Improving Decisions About Health, Wealth, and Happiness

Week 28

Scenario #28: You're in the grocery line. There is a couple in front of you. The man keeps trying to grab the woman's buttocks. The woman keeps swatting him away, telling him to "stop" as she looks around to see who's watching, ashamed.

What could you think, say or do in this situation, to all those involved, that would pull you away from being your very best self?

The Victim	
Witnesses	
The Harasser	
HR/Supervisor	

What could you think, say or do in this situation, to all those involved, that would enable you to fully bloom?

 The Victim 	
 Witnesses 	
 The Harasser 	
 HR/Supervisor 	

What knowledge, skills and abilities (K.S.A.s) do you have already, and which do you need to learn, acquire and grow to be your best self in this scenario?

1. Be impeccable with your word
2. Don't take anything personally
3. Don't make assumptions
4. Always do your best

Don Miguel Ruiz
The Four Agreements: A Toltec Wisdom Book

Week 29

Scenario #29: You and your colleagues from work are attending a formal event. One of your female colleagues wearing a low-cut dress with lots of cleavage makes a point of bending over at the waist when she says hello to the boss.

What could you think, say or do in this situation, to all those involved, that would pull you away from being your very best self?

The Victim	
Witnesses	
The Harasser	
HR/Supervisor	

What could you think, say or do in this situation, to all those involved, that would enable you to fully bloom?

The Victim	
Witnesses	
The Harasser	
HR/Supervisor	

What knowledge, skills and abilities (K.S.A.s) do you have already, and which do you need to learn, acquire and grow to be your best self in this scenario?

"Conflict cannot survive without your participation."

Wayne Dyer
Philosopher, Self-Help Author, and Motivational Speaker

Week 30

Scenario #30: You and the women in the office are out to lunch and a few of them start talking playfully about how hot two of your male colleagues are and what they would like to "do" with them.

What could you think, say or do in this situation, to all those involved, that would pull you away from being your very best self?

The Victim	
Witnesses	
The Harasser	
HR/Supervisor	

What could you think, say or do in this situation, to all those involved, that would enable you to fully bloom?

The Victim	
Witnesses	
The Harasser	
HR/Supervisor	

What knowledge, skills and abilities (K.S.A.s) do you have already, and which do you need to learn, acquire and grow to be your best self in this scenario?

"I have always found that mercy bears richer fruits
than strict justice."

Abraham Lincoln
American statesman and lawyer,
16th President of the United States (March, 1861- April, 1865)

Week 31

Scenario #31: You are the supervisor of a 30-person mixed gender team. You overhear some of the men expressing frustration with the #MeToo movement. You've seen some of the women at some of the Women's March events.

What could you think, say or do in this situation, to all those involved, that would pull you away from being your very best self?

The Victim	
Witnesses	
The Harasser	
HR/Supervisor	

What could you think, say or do in this situation, to all those involved, that would enable you to fully bloom?

The Victim	
Witnesses	
The Harasser	
HR/Supervisor	

What knowledge, skills and abilities (K.S.A.s) do you have already, and which do you need to learn, acquire and grow to be your best self in this scenario?

"You may encounter many defeats, but you must not be defeated.
In fact, it may be necessary to encounter the defeats,
so you can know who you are, what you can rise from,
how you can still come out of it."

Maya Angelou
American Poet, Singer, Memoirist, and Civil Rights Activist

Week 32

Scenario #32: You know one of the women in your office is receiving a lot of attention from one of the men in the office. He wants to take her out on a date. She wants nothing to do with him. He persists.

What could you think, say or do in this situation, to all those involved, that would pull you away from being your very best self?

The Victim	
Witnesses	
The Harasser	
HR/Supervisor	

What could you think, say or do in this situation, to all those involved, that would enable you to fully bloom?

The Victim	
Witnesses	
The Harasser	
HR/Supervisor	

What knowledge, skills and abilities (K.S.A.s) do you have already, and which do you need to learn, acquire and grow to be your best self in this scenario?

"It is from the numberless diverse acts of
courage and belief that human history is shaped.
Each time a man stands up for an ideal
or acts to improve the lot of others or strikes out against injustice,
he sends forth a tiny ripple of hope, and crossing each other
from a million different centers of energy and daring,
those ripples build a current that can sweep down
the mightiest walls of oppression and resistance."

Robert Kennedy
United States Senator and Lawyer

Week 33

Scenario #33: The wives come in to raise funds for a colleague with cancer. They want the men in the office to do a "Beach Boys" calendar and have all the men pose in bathing suits.

What could you think, say or do in this situation, to all those involved, that would pull you away from being your very best self?

The Victim	
Witnesses	
The Harasser	
HR/Supervisor	

What could you think, say or do in this situation, to all those involved, that would enable you to fully bloom?

The Victim	
Witnesses	
The Harasser	
HR/Supervisor	

What knowledge, skills and abilities (K.S.A.s) do you have already, and which do you need to learn, acquire and grow to be your best self in this scenario?

"Power can be taken, but not given.
The process of the taking is empowerment in itself."

Gloria Steinem
American Feminist, Journalist, Social Political Activist, and Leader

Week 34

Scenario #34: A new, younger, hotter co-worker is hired and all the unwanted attention you have been receiving now focuses on her.

What could you think, say or do in this situation, to all those involved, that would pull you away from being your very best self?

The Victim	
Witnesses	
The Harasser	
HR/Supervisor	

What could you think, say or do in this situation, to all those involved, that would enable you to fully bloom?

The Victim	
Witnesses	
The Harasser	
HR/Supervisor	

What knowledge, skills and abilities (K.S.A.s) do you have already, and which do you need to learn, acquire and grow to be your best self in this scenario?

"A woman is like a tea bag –
you can't tell how strong she is until you put her in hot water."

Eleanor Roosevelt
American Politician, Diplomat, Activist and
First Lady of the United States (March 1933 - April 1945)

Week 35

Scenario #35: It's hot out on the flight deck, close to 100°. One of the ensigns is 8 months pregnant, in uniform and looking worn down by the heat. The unit leader, a lieutenant, tells her to suck it up and press on.

What could you think, say or do in this situation, to all those involved, that would pull you away from being your very best self?

The Victim	
Witnesses	
The Harasser	
HR/Supervisor	

What could you think, say or do in this situation, to all those involved, that would enable you to fully bloom?

 The Victim	
 Witnesses	
 The Harasser	
 HR/Supervisor	

What knowledge, skills and abilities (K.S.A.s) do you have already, and which do you need to learn, acquire and grow to be your best self in this scenario?

"Listen to what you know instead of what you fear."

Richard Bach
Author
Jonathan Livingston Seagull

Week 36

Scenario #36: You go out to lunch and see a group of co-workers from your floor eating together across the room. One of the male colleagues has ordered the ribs. As the others are chatting, he catches the eye of the young intern and eats the meat off the bone suggestively. She watches initially, then quickly looks away.

What could you think, say or do in this situation, to all those involved, that would pull you away from being your very best self?

The Victim	
Witnesses	
The Harasser	
HR/Supervisor	

What could you think, say or do in this situation, to all those involved, that would enable you to fully bloom?

The Victim	
Witnesses	
The Harasser	
HR/Supervisor	

What knowledge, skills and abilities (K.S.A.s) do you have already, and which do you need to learn, acquire and grow to be your best self in this scenario?

"It is easier to prevent bad habits than to break them."

Benjamin Franklin
Author, Scientist, Statesman, Polymath
and one of the Founding Fathers of the United States

Week 37

Scenario #37: You overhear the guys on the team talk about their plans to put the new gal in the lead role for debriefing the client because he likes hot women and the news in the debrief is bad. He would be more receptive hearing the news from her than from them.

What could you think, say or do in this situation, to all those involved, that would pull you away from being your very best self?

The Victim	
Witnesses	
The Harasser	
HR/Supervisor	

What could you think, say or do in this situation, to all those involved, that would enable you to fully bloom?

The Victim	
Witnesses	
The Harasser	
HR/Supervisor	

What knowledge, skills and abilities (K.S.A.s) do you have already, and which do you need to learn, acquire and grow to be your best self in this scenario?

"The most difficult thing is the decision to act,
the rest is merely tenacity. The fears are paper tigers.
You can do anything you decide to do. You can act to change and
control your life; and the procedure, the process is its own reward."

Amelia Earhart
American Aviation Pioneer, Author

Week 38

Scenario #38: A friend is driving you home and gets pulled over for speeding. The cop starts to flirt with your friend and suggests that for a date with her, he will let her off with just a warning.

What could you think, say or do in this situation, to all those involved, that would pull you away from being your very best self?

The Victim	
Witnesses	
The Harasser	
HR/Supervisor	

What could you think, say or do in this situation, to all those
involved, that would enable you to fully bloom?

The Victim	
Witnesses	
The Harasser	
HR/Supervisor	

What knowledge, skills and abilities (K.S.A.s) do you have already, and
which do you need to learn, acquire and grow to be your best self in
this scenario?

"Each person holds so much power within themselves that needs to be let out. Sometimes they just need a little nudge, a little direction, a little support, a little coaching, and the greatest things can happen."

Pete Carroll
Football Coach and Executive Vice President

Week 39

Scenario #39: There's one guy in the office that has a pet name for all the women in the office, but not for the men.

What could you think, say or do in this situation, to all those involved, that would pull you away from being your very best self?

The Victim	
Witnesses	
The Harasser	
HR/Supervisor	

What could you think, say or do in this situation, to all those involved, that would enable you to fully bloom?

The Victim	
Witnesses	
The Harasser	
HR/Supervisor	

What knowledge, skills and abilities (K.S.A.s) do you have already, and which do you need to learn, acquire and grow to be your best self in this scenario?

"A creative man is motivated by the desire to achieve, not by the desire to beat others."

Ayn Rand
Russian-American Novelist, Philosopher,
Playwright and Screenwriter

Week 40

Scenario #40: You offer to help a female buddy work late on a deadline. Unaware you are there, the boss walks in, crosses the room and begins to rub her shoulders. You think, but you're not sure, that she is uncomfortable with this touching. You certainly are.

What could you think, say or do in this situation, to all those involved, that would pull you away from being your very best self?

The Victim	
Witnesses	
The Harasser	
HR/Supervisor	

What could you think, say or do in this situation, to all those involved, that would enable you to fully bloom?

The Victim	
Witnesses	
The Harasser	
HR/Supervisor	

What knowledge, skills and abilities (K.S.A.s) do you have already, and which do you need to learn, acquire and grow to be your best self in this scenario?

"Every social justice movement that I know of has come out of people sitting in small groups, telling their life stories, and discovering that other people have shared similar experiences."

Gloria Steinem
American Feminist, Journalist, Social Political Activist, and Leader

Gathering

Find 2 or 3 friends to go on this journal journey with you.
Once a quarter, or after every 12 weeks, I invite you to pause your
introspection and reconnect with those in your trusted circle.
Plan a meal together, host a Gathering and
open up about your "Getting Ready" experience so far.

Scenario #41a: How are you "ready" to deal with and heal from these scenarios – physically, emotionally, socially, intellectually, and spiritually? What KSAs have you mastered already?

Physical

Emotional

Social

Intellectual

Spiritual

Scenario #41b: In which petals do you still have some "getting ready" work to do? What are the common growth areas? Can someone's strengths help someone else grow? What is your plan for growth?

Physical

Emotional

Social

Intellectual

Spiritual

"The real man smiles in trouble, gathers strength from distress, and grows brave by reflection."

Thomas Paine
English-born American Political Activist,
Philosopher, Political Theorist, Revolutionary
and one of the Founding Fathers of the United States

Week 42

Scenario #42: Every time you go into your male colleague's office he quickly closes a computer screen he has open. This time you catch a glimpse of lingerie before the screen closes. He looks threateningly at you when he sees that you saw this.

What could you think, say or do in this situation, to all those involved, that would pull you away from being your very best self?

The Victim	
Witnesses	
The Harasser	
HR/Supervisor	

What could you think, say or do in this situation, to all those involved, that would enable you to fully bloom?

The Victim	
Witnesses	
The Harasser	
HR/Supervisor	

What knowledge, skills and abilities (K.S.A.s) do you have already, and which do you need to learn, acquire and grow to be your best self in this scenario?

"You gain strength, courage, and confidence
by every experience in which you really stop to look fear in the face.
You are able to say to yourself, 'I lived through this horror.
I can take the next thing that comes along.' "

Eleanor Roosevelt
American Politician, Diplomat, Activist and
First Lady of the United States (March 1933 - April 1945)

Week 43

Scenario #43: You do your work and you do it well. Unfortunately, that means you do it better than your male office-mate and he hates you for it. One day, after hours, he corners you in the breakroom, overpowers you and begins to assault you. He tears your blouse off, sending buttons everywhere, and almost rips your pants off when a noise in the hallway stops him.

What could you think, say or do in this situation, to all those involved, that would pull you away from being your very best self?

The Victim	
Witnesses	
The Harasser	
HR/Supervisor	

What could you think, say or do in this situation, to all those involved, that would enable you to fully bloom?

  The Victim	
  Witnesses	
  The Harasser	
  HR/Supervisor	

What knowledge, skills and abilities (K.S.A.s) do you have already, and which do you need to learn, acquire and grow to be your best self in this scenario?

"Human greatness does not lie in wealth or power, but in character and goodness. People are just people, and all people have faults and shortcomings, but all of us are born with a basic goodness."

Anne Frank
German-born Diarist, and Jewish Victim of the Holocaust whose story is told in *The Diary of a Young Girl*

Week 44

Scenario #44: You are torn between filing a sexual harassment report and just enduring the humiliation, when a promotion opportunity comes your way. This would move you away from your harasser but the person replacing you might be another woman.

What could you think, say or do in this situation, to all those involved, that would pull you away from being your very best self?

The Victim	
Witnesses	
The Harasser	
HR/Supervisor	

What could you think, say or do in this situation, to all those involved, that would enable you to fully bloom?

The Victim	
Witnesses	
The Harasser	
HR/Supervisor	

What knowledge, skills and abilities (K.S.A.s) do you have already, and which do you need to learn, acquire and grow to be your best self in this scenario?

"What you do today can improve all your tomorrows."

Ralph Marston
Writer

Week 45

Scenario #45: You have already filed a sexual harassment report with HR about your male office-mate. They say that the report is anonymous and for you to go back to work as normal. But when the company takes action, he corners you one day and demands to know if it was you that snitched.

What could you think, say or do in this situation, to all those involved, that would pull you away from being your very best self?

The Victim	
Witnesses	
The Harasser	
HR/Supervisor	

What could you think, say or do in this situation, to all those involved, that would enable you to fully bloom?

The Victim	
Witnesses	
The Harasser	
HR/Supervisor	

What knowledge, skills and abilities (K.S.A.s) do you have already, and which do you need to learn, acquire and grow to be your best self in this scenario?

"A little consideration, a little thought for others,
makes all the difference."

Winnie-the-Pooh
The best bear in all the world
A.A. Milne

Week 46

Scenario #46: Your supervisor is a member of the old boys' club and is not happy that he has to protect you from retaliation for the sexual harassment report you submitted on your office-mate. He subtly belittles you every chance he gets.

What could you think, say or do in this situation, to all those involved, that would pull you away from being your very best self?

The Victim	
Witnesses	
The Harasser	
HR/Supervisor	

What could you think, say or do in this situation, to all those involved, that would enable you to fully bloom?

 The Victim	
 Witnesses	
 The Harasser	
 HR/Supervisor	

What knowledge, skills and abilities (K.S.A.s) do you have already, and which do you need to learn, acquire and grow to be your best self in this scenario?

"Only I can change my life. No one can do it for me."

Carol Burnett
American Actress, Comedian, Singer and Writer

Week 47

Scenario #47: Since you filed your sexual harassment report, your office-mate has been on his best behavior. But you get a bad feeling when his office buddies use odd phrases, look at you a little differently, and find subtle but legitimate reasons to keep you off their projects.

What could you think, say or do in this situation, to all those involved, that would pull you away from being your very best self?

The Victim	
Witnesses	
The Harasser	
HR/Supervisor	

What could you think, say or do in this situation, to all those involved, that would enable you to fully bloom?

The Victim	
Witnesses	
The Harasser	
HR/Supervisor	

What knowledge, skills and abilities (K.S.A.s) do you have already, and which do you need to learn, acquire and grow to be your best self in this scenario?

"I would rather go to any extreme
than suffer anything that is unworthy of my reputation,
or of that of my crown."

Queen Elizabeth I
Queen of England and Ireland (November, 1558 – March, 1603)

Week 48

Scenario #48: You have followed all the advice in the sexual harassment training videos but three months after you filed your report, nothing has changed. He is still harassing you.

What could you think, say or do in this situation, to all those involved, that would pull you away from being your very best self?

The Victim	
Witnesses	
The Harasser	
HR/Supervisor	

What could you think, say or do in this situation, to all those involved, that would enable you to fully bloom?

The Victim	
Witnesses	
The Harasser	
HR/Supervisor	

What knowledge, skills and abilities (K.S.A.s) do you have already, and which do you need to learn, acquire and grow to be your best self in this scenario?

"Character cannot be developed in ease and quiet.
Only through experience of trial and suffering can the soul be
strengthened, ambition inspired, and success achieved."

Helen Keller
Author, Political Activist, Lecturer

Week 49

Scenario #49: Your office is investigating your sexual harassment report along with the handful of other reports they have received. You are called into HR. The men in the office stand at the edge of their cubicles and in their office doorways and watch you walk to the elevator, all while seeming to have a legitimate reason to chat with each other.

What could you think, say or do in this situation, to all those involved, that would pull you away from being your very best self?

The Victim	
Witnesses	
The Harasser	
HR/Supervisor	

What could you think, say or do in this situation, to all those involved, that would enable you to fully bloom?

The Victim	
Witnesses	
The Harasser	
HR/Supervisor	

What knowledge, skills and abilities (K.S.A.s) do you have already, and which do you need to learn, acquire and grow to be your best self in this scenario?

"No one saves us but ourselves.
No one can and no one may.
We ourselves must walk the path."

Buddha
Siddhārtha Gautama Shakyamuni Buddha

Week 50

Scenario #50: HR hasn't helped. You have taken your sexual harassment claim to the Equal Employment Opportunity Commission (EEOC) for mediation. After 3 hours of mediating, the company offers you $10,000 in damages and a modest severance package. Your $450/hr. lawyer asks you whether you want to accept the offer. You have already used up your $5000 retainer.

What could you think, say or do in this situation, to all those involved, that would pull you away from being your very best self?

The Victim	
Witnesses	
The Harasser	
HR/Supervisor	

What could you think, say or do in this situation, to all those involved, that would enable you to fully bloom?

 The Victim 	
 Witnesses 	
 The Harasser 	
 HR/Supervisor 	

What knowledge, skills and abilities (K.S.A.s) do you have already, and which do you need to learn, acquire and grow to be your best self in this scenario?

"You have power over your mind - not outside events.
Realize this, and you will find strength."

Marcus Aurelius
Roman Emperor (161 AD to 180 AD), Stoic Philosopher and Author
Meditations

Week 51

Scenario #51: Your office just lost one of its workers as a result of a sexual harassment case. The harasser is still in the office, though reassigned to a new department. The victim has moved on. While no one knows the whole story, everyone in the office is guessing what happened.

What could you think, say or do in this situation, to all those involved, that would pull you away from being your very best self?

The Victim	
Witnesses	
The Harasser	
HR/Supervisor	

What could you think, say or do in this situation, to all those involved, that would enable you to fully bloom?

The Victim	
Witnesses	
The Harasser	
HR/Supervisor	

What knowledge, skills and abilities (K.S.A.s) do you have already, and which do you need to learn, acquire and grow to be your best self in this scenario?

"Let her sleep, for tomorrow, she will shake the world."

Napoleon Buonaparte
Military Leader, French Statesman and
Emperor of the French (May 1804 – April 1814)

Week 52

Scenario #52: Your office just lost one of its workers as a result of a sexual harassment case. The victim is still in the office, though reassigned to a new department. The harasser has moved on. While no one knows the whole story, everyone in the office is guessing what happened.

What could you think, say or do in this situation, to all those involved, that would pull you away from being your very best self?

The Victim	
Witnesses	
The Harasser	
HR/Supervisor	

What could you think, say or do in this situation, to all those involved, that would enable you to fully bloom?

 The Victim	
 Witnesses	
 The Harasser	
 HR/Supervisor	

What knowledge, skills and abilities (K.S.A.s) do you have already, and which do you need to learn, acquire and grow to be your best self in this scenario?

"A friend is one that knows you as you are,
understands where you have been, accepts what you have become, and
still, gently allows you to grow."

William Shakespeare
English Poet, Playwright and Actor

Gathering

Find 2 or 3 friends to go on this journal journey with you.
Once a quarter, or after every 12 weeks, I invite you to pause your
introspection and reconnect with those in your trusted circle.
Plan a meal together, host a Gathering and
open up about your "Getting Ready" experience so far.

Scenario #53a: How are you "ready" to deal with and heal from these scenarios – physically, emotionally, socially, intellectually, and spiritually? What KSAs have you mastered already?

Physical

Emotional

Social

Intellectual

Spiritual

Scenario #53b: In which petals do you still have some "getting ready" work to do? What are the common growth areas? Can someone's strengths help someone else grow? What is your plan for growth?

Physical

Emotional

Social

Intellectual

Spiritual

"Follow effective action with quiet reflection.
From the quiet reflection will come even more effective action."

Peter Drucker
Management Consultant, Educator, and Author

Summing Up

"Let me explain... No, there is too much. Let me sum up.
Buttercup is marrying Humperdinck in a little less than half an hour, so
all we have to do is get in, break up the wedding,
steal the Princess, and make our escape..."

Inigo Montoya
The Princess Bride
By William Goldman

Looking back on your year of reflections and gatherings, what are your main strengths that you practice regularly to "stay ready" for any sexual harassment scenario?

Physical

Emotional

Social

Intellectual

Spiritual

Looking back on your year of reflections and gatherings, what are your main weaknesses that you need to develop in order to "get ready" for any sexual harassment scenario? What is your plan for that growth?

Physical

Emotional

Social

Intellectual

Spiritual

About the Author

Sara Jones is the founder of Plum Blossom Creations, a San Diego-based firm invested in the growth of people and small businesses. Having been there and done that, she writes a blog called Stories from Athena's Garden (www.storiesfromathenasgarden.com) to start the discussion on ways to deal with and heal from sexual harassment and the retaliation that often comes from standing up against it.

Ms. Jones holds a B.A. in Renaissance Studies from Yale University, an M.Ed. from Harvard's Graduate School of Education, in Administration, Planning and Social Policy, an MBA from UCSD's Rady School of Management and a 1st degree Black Belt in the art of Go Zan Ryu Tengu Ninjitsu. A native of San Diego, she has lived in the U.S., France and Brazil and has traveled to Western Europe, New Zealand, Australia, Mexico, Peru, Chile, Argentina, Japan and China. She is a daughter, sister, aunt and friend. She has been an educator, emergency manager and marketing executive as well as a volunteer with the American Red Cross and the U.S. Coast Guard Auxiliary.

A life-long learner, she continues to teach and help people get from where they are to where they want or need to be. In her spare time, she swims in the ocean and hikes the trails that rise up to meet her. This is her first book.

Acknowledgements

Thank you to the handful of people that helped with this project. Thank you, Kimberly Tilton, (ktiltonphotoart.com) for the lovely photo of me and your help in copy editing. Thank you, Laura Van Tyne, for your helpful advice to put it in print and to Freepik (www.flaticon.com) for the icons.

Share Your Story

www.storiesfromathenasgarden.com/share-your-story

If you are on this journey and can offer your story, we welcome your voice. By telling your story, not only do you heal yourself, but you help others learn what they *should have* and *could have* done, and how your life *would have* been different if they had, instead of what they chose to do. Please do.

Share Your Resources

www.storiesfromathenasgarden.com/share-your-resources

If you are on this journey, you know how important it is to have the right resources to enable your success and the success of others also on this journey. If you can offer your resources to others, please do. Here are just some of the resource categories that we know are needed to help each of our 5 petals bloom.

- Advocates, Speakers, & Trainers
- Books and Movies
- Companies in Full Bloom
- Financial Planners & Services
- Flower Shops
- Groups, Support Groups
- Healers
- Health and Wellness Professionals
- Health, Fitness & the Great Outdoors
- HR Consultants
- Inspiration and Insights
- International Resources
- Life Coaches
- Mental Health Professionals
- National Resources
- Self-Care Professionals

Plum Blossom Creations, LLC
San Diego, CA
www.plumblossomcreations.com

CPSIA information can be obtained
at www.ICGtesting.com
Printed in the USA
FSHW02n2042250518
48585FS